# GET MY SH$T TOGETHER
## *Journal*

### LAURYN ENGLAND

© Copyright 2020 by Jaylon Aaron White &
Dr. Synovia Dover-Harris
Printed in the USA by A2Z Books, LLC. All rights reserved. This book or any portion thereof may not be reproduced or used in any manner whatsoever without the express written permission of the publisher except for the use of brief quotations in book review
Printed in the United Stated.
First Printing ISBN 978-1-943284-61-0
www.A2ZBookspublishing.net

# Welcome to The
## *Get My Sh$T Together*
# JOURNAL

Hi I am Jaylon Aaron also known as Lauryn England. Over the past few years I have found myself struggling with different aspects of my life. I struggled with relationships both personal and professional. I struggled with money and credit. I always struggled with my self-image. My sexuality is always a problem for someone and through all of this, I found myself being very depressed. Some days I didn't know rather I was going or coming and even had thoughts of suicide. I knew that the road I was going down wasn't leading me anywhere, but destruction. So, I knew I needed to make some dramatic changes. I got rid of all the negative energy & toxic people. I started journaling and having faith. I started holding myself accountable for the bad decisions I was making it my life and decided to stop making them. And believe it or not within a few weeks of me doing these things my life started turning around.

We all know that in life bad things will happen, but the way you deal with them is the deciding factor on if you will be happy and successful or not. I created this Journal to help everyone create a life that is pleasing to them by Getting Their Sh$T Together.

Lauryn England

## This Journal Belongs To

_____

_____

_____

> ❝
> *We may encounter many defeats but we must not be defeated.*
>
> Maya Angelou

# In What Areas of My Life Do I Need to *Get My Sh$t together?*

- ☐ Finances
- ☐ Relationships
- ☐ Business
- ☐ School
- ☐ Weight
- ☐ Credit
- ☐ Mental
- ☐ Love
- ☐ Family
- ☐ Other (write what applies to you)

_____

_____

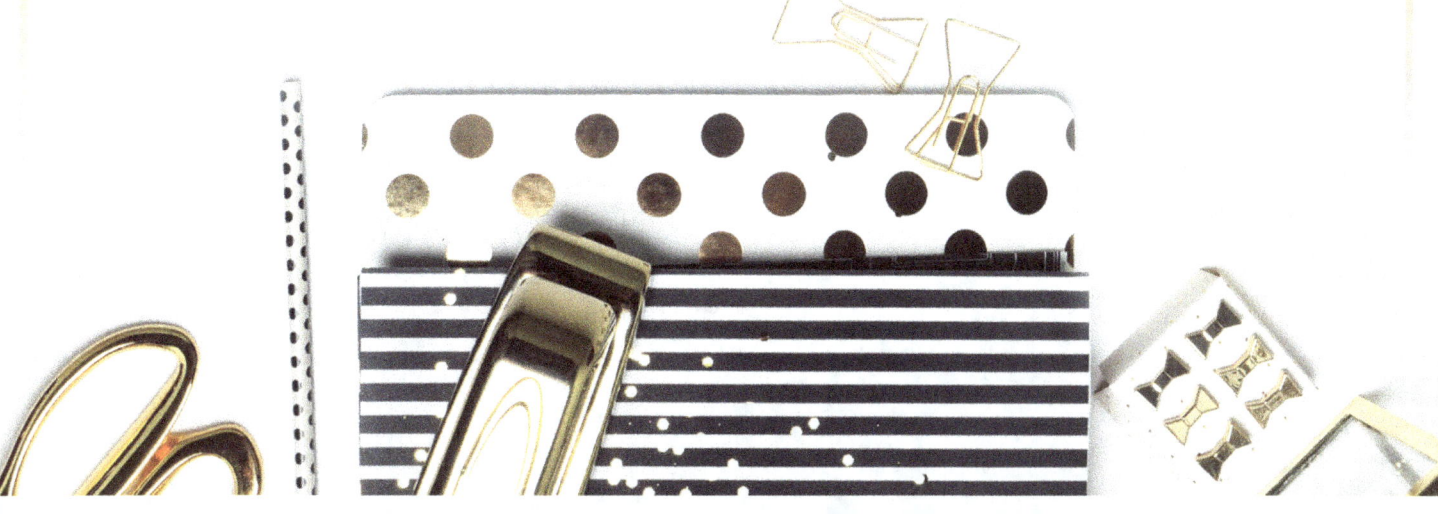

> **Start where you are.
> Use what you have.
> *Do what you can.***
>
> Arthur Ashe

# 1st Quarter

# What Sh$T do you need to get together this Quarter?

For example:
- I need to fix my credit.
- I want to get out of depression.
- I want to build a better relationship with my mom.
- I want to lose 20lbs.

# What are the Steps to Getting my Sh$T Together this Quarter?

For example:
- I need to contact that credit company I saw on Instagram.
- I need to go to a physcologist.
- I will call start calling my mom once I week.
- I will stop eating sweets this month.

_____
_____
_____
_____
_____
_____
_____
_____
_____
_____
_____
_____

# What is my Motivation this Quarter to Get My Sh$t Together?

For example:
- I want to buy a house.
- I want to get married.
- I want to start spending Holidays at my parents' house.
- I am going on a girls trip.

_____
_____
_____
_____
_____
_____
_____
_____
_____
_____
_____
_____
_____
_____
_____
_____
_____

# Get My Sh$T Together Word Search

Use this word search puzzle as a way to relax yourself.

## Success

```
L J P C Z A M Q G B F H E O H Y R O T C I V M
E I Y L O D N L A E L E V N P Y T R M Q Y P U
R L C U X V O W I D Y N W T P S N E T K P R T
E K N T E A F Y N O I U A R B E E V I G R O T
H A A K M N G N D F N T L A E N M O E P E F R
G R D S A C M O R R G R K E N S N L P R A I I
U R N S F E L I A O C O A A E A I C R W L T U
A I E E L I L T W S O F W S F T A E O A I O M
L V C N K P E A E E L T A Y I I T J G L Z N P
N A S I I X W R R S O I Y S T O T Z R K A K H
Y L A P L N O U S X R H Z T D N A A E O T S X
V W P P L I D T E L S G D R O F Q P S V I T F
V H A A I W T A S T R I K E I R H C S E O F A
A I N H N M A M R W K B B E N Y Y N V R N V T
S T S M G V P B M K N O I T I U R F X B S H N
P R O S P E R I T Y E M I N E N C E B O O M D
```

Find the following words in the puzzle.

| | | | |
|---|---|---|---|
| FLYINGCOLORS | SENSATION | ]BENEFIT | BIGHIT |
| REALIZATION | WALKAWAY | VICTORY | DOWELL |
| ATTAINMENT | PROGRESS | TRIUMPH | SAVVY |
| ASCENDANCY | EMINENCE | FORTUNE | GAIN |
| MATURATION | WALKOVER | ARRIVAL | FAME |
| PROSPERITY | FRUITION | REWARD | BOOM |
| BEDOFROSES | LAUGHER | CLOVER | SNAP |
| EASYSTREET | KILLING | STRIKE | WIN |
| HAPPINESS | ADVANCE | PROFIT | HIT |

**Month:** _____

| SUNDAY | MONDAY | TUESDAY | WEDNESDAY |
|---|---|---|---|
| | | | |
| | | | |
| | | | |
| | | | |
| | | | |

| THURSDAY | FRIDAY | SATURDAY |
|----------|--------|----------|
|          |        |          |
|          |        |          |
|          |        |          |
|          |        |          |
|          |        |          |

## Notes

# THIS MONTH'S AFFIRMATION

## I will Step Out on Faith

### Rewrite & Site

_____

_____

_____

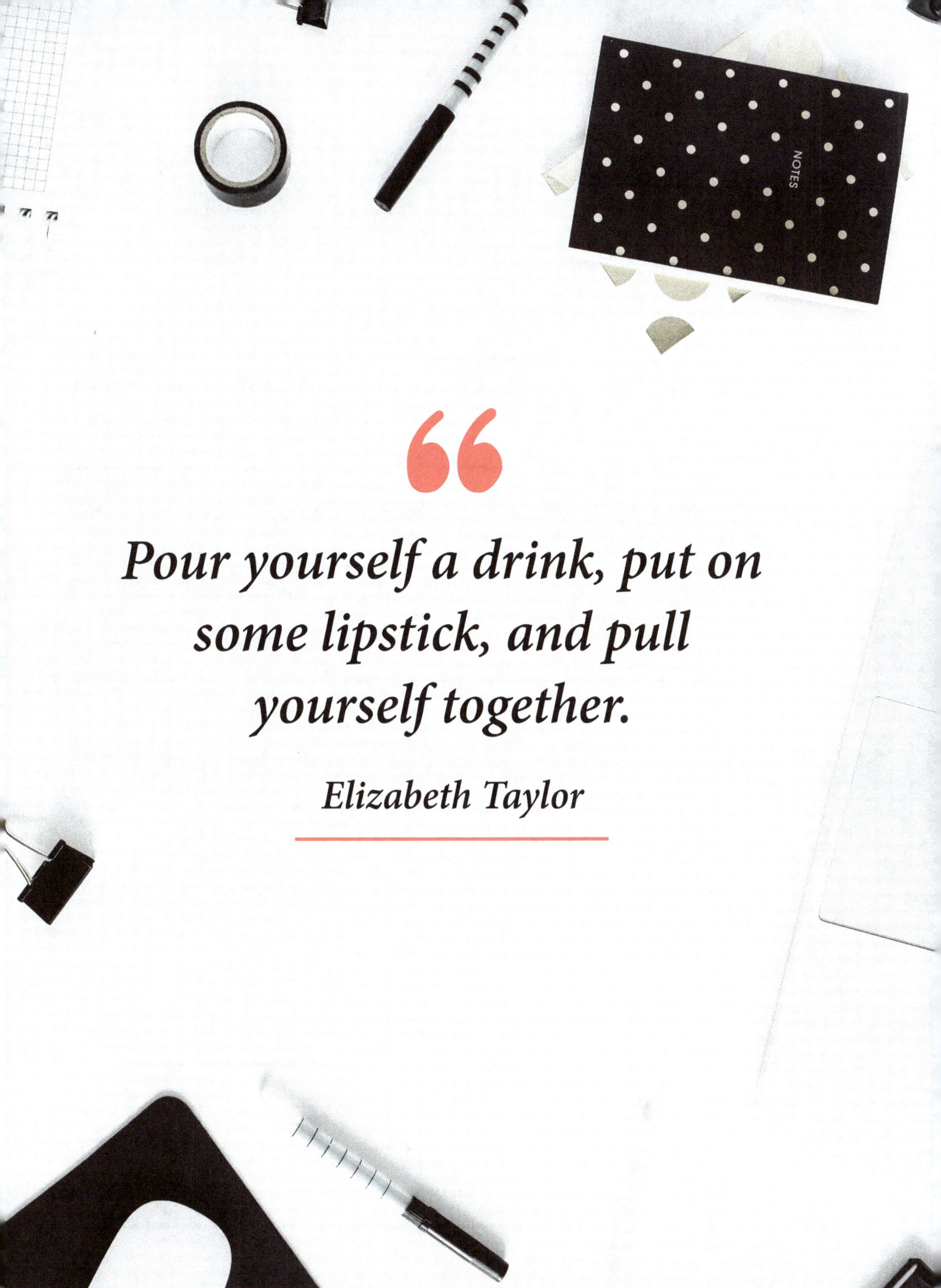

> *Pour yourself a drink, put on some lipstick, and pull yourself together.*
>
> Elizabeth Taylor

# Journal Here

(Journaling is a practice utilized to ease the mind, reduce stress and anxiety.)
Write What's on Your Mind

_____
_____
_____
_____
_____
_____
_____
_____
_____
_____
_____
_____
_____
_____
_____
_____
_____

# Journal Here

(Journaling is a practice utilized to ease the mind, reduce stress and anxiety.)
Write What's on Your Mind

_____
_____
_____
_____
_____
_____
_____
_____
_____
_____
_____
_____
_____
_____
_____
_____
_____

# Get My Sh$t Together Vision Board

(Place images or words here that will motivate you to Get your Sh$t together this month)

Month: _____

| SUNDAY | MONDAY | TUESDAY | WEDNESDAY |
|--------|--------|---------|-----------|
|        |        |         |           |
|        |        |         |           |
|        |        |         |           |
|        |        |         |           |
|        |        |         |           |

| THURSDAY | FRIDAY | SATURDAY |
|---|---|---|
| | | |
| | | |
| | | |
| | | |
| | | |

## Notes

## THIS MONTH'S AFFIRMATION

## *I Will Accomplish My Goals*

### Rewrite & Site

_____

_____

_____

> **Life is 10% what happens to you and 90% how you react to it.**
>
> Charles R. Swindoll

# Journal Here

(Journaling is a practice utilized to ease the mind, reduce stress and anxiety.)
Write What's on Your Mind

_____
_____
_____
_____
_____
_____
_____
_____
_____
_____
_____
_____
_____
_____
_____

# Journal Here

(Journaling is a practice utilized to ease the mind, reduce stress and anxiety.)
Write What's on Your Mind

_____
_____
_____
_____
_____
_____
_____
_____
_____
_____
_____
_____
_____
_____
_____
_____
_____

# Get My Sh$t Together Vision Board

(Place images or words here that will motivate you to Get your Sh$t together this month)

# Midquarter Get My Sh$T Together Accountability Checklist

Am I on track to Getting My Sh$t together this month?
_____
_____
_____
_____
_____
_____

If yes, what am I doing?
_____
_____
_____
_____
_____
_____

If no what changes do I need to make?
_____
_____
_____
_____
_____
_____
_____

Month: _____

| SUNDAY | MONDAY | TUESDAY | WEDNESDAY |
|--------|--------|---------|-----------|
|        |        |         |           |
|        |        |         |           |
|        |        |         |           |
|        |        |         |           |
|        |        |         |           |

| THURSDAY | FRIDAY | SATURDAY |
|---|---|---|
| | | |
| | | |
| | | |
| | | |
| | | |

## Notes

# THIS MONTH'S AFFIRMATION

## *I Will Not Allow Anyone or Anything To Get in the Way of Me Accomplishing My Goals*

## Rewrite & Site

_____

_____

> *Only I can change my life.
> No one can do it for me.*
>
> — Carol Burnett

# Journal Here

(Journaling is a practice utilized to ease the mind, reduce stress and anxiety.)
Write What's on Your Mind

_____
_____
_____
_____
_____
_____
_____
_____
_____
_____
_____
_____
_____
_____
_____
_____

# Journal Here

(Journaling is a practice utilized to ease the mind, reduce stress and anxiety.)
Write What's on Your Mind

_____
_____
_____
_____
_____
_____
_____
_____
_____
_____
_____
_____
_____
_____
_____
_____
_____
_____
_____

# Get My Sh$t Together Vision Board

(Place images or words here that will motivate you to Get your Sh$t together this month)

# 2nd Quarter

# What Sh$T do you need to get together this Quarter?

For example:
- I need to fix my credit.
- I want to get out of depression.
- I want to build a better relationship with my mom.
- I want to lose 20lbs.

_____
_____
_____
_____
_____
_____
_____
_____
_____
_____
_____
_____
_____
_____

# What are the Steps to Getting my Sh$T Together this Quarter?

For example:
- I need to contact that credit company I saw on Instagram.
- I need to go to a physcologist.
- I will call start calling my mom once I week.
- I will stop eating sweets this month.

_____
_____
_____
_____
_____
_____
_____
_____
_____
_____
_____
_____

# What is my Motivation this Quarter to Get My Sh$t Together?

For example:
- I want to buy a house.
- I want to get married.
- I want to start spending Holidays at my parents' house.
- I am going on a girls trip.

# Get My Sh$T Together Word Search

Use this word search puzzle as a way to relax yourself.

## Achieve

```
L J P C Z A M Q G B F H E O H Y R O T C I V M
E I Y L O D N L A E L E V N P Y T R M Q Y P U
R L C U X V O W I D Y N W T P S N E T K P R T
E K N T E A F Y N O I U A R B E E V I G R O T
H A A K M N G N D F N T L A E N M O E P E F R
G R D S A C M O R R G R K E N S N L P R A I I
U R N S F E L I A O C O A A E A I C R W L T U
A I E E L I T W S O F W S F T A E O A I O M
L V C N K P E A E E L T A Y I I T J G L Z N P
N A S I I X W R R S O I Y S T O T Z R K A K H
Y L A P L N O U S X R H Z T D N A A E O T S X
V W P P L I D T E L S G D R O F Q P S V I T F
V H A A I W T A S T R I K E I R H C S E O F A
A I N H N M A M R W K B B E N Y Y N V R N V T
S T S M G V P B M K N O I T I U R F X B S H N
P R O S P E R I T Y E M I N E N C E B O O M D
```

Find the following words in the puzzle.

| | | | | |
|---|---|---|---|---|
| ACCOMPLISH | COMPLETE | GETDONE | FINISH | SCORE |
| EFFECTUATE | BRINGOFF | RESOLVE | MANAGE | EARN |
| BRINGABOUT | CARRYOUT | FULFILL | EFFECT | SIGN |
| ACTUALIZE | EXECUTE | WORKOUT | WINDUP | GAIN |
| EARNWINGS | PROCURE | DELIVER | SETTLE | SEAL |
| NEGOTIATE | PERFORM | ACQUIRE | CLOSE | WIN |
| DISCHARGE | PRODUCE | OBTAIN | SOLVE | END |
| CONCLUDE | PERFECT | ATTAIN | REACH | GET |
| DISPATCH | REALIZE | RACKUP | ENACT | CAP |
| | | | | DO |

Month: _____

| SUNDAY | MONDAY | TUESDAY | WEDNESDAY |
|--------|--------|---------|-----------|
|        |        |         |           |
|        |        |         |           |
|        |        |         |           |
|        |        |         |           |
|        |        |         |           |

| THURSDAY | FRIDAY | SATURDAY |
|---|---|---|
| | | |
| | | |
| | | |
| | | |
| | | |

Notes

# THIS MONTH'S AFFIRMATION

## I Will Live the life of my Dreams

### Rewrite & Site

_____

_____

_____

> *Good, better, best. Never let it rest. 'Til your good is better and your better is best.*
>
> St. Jerome

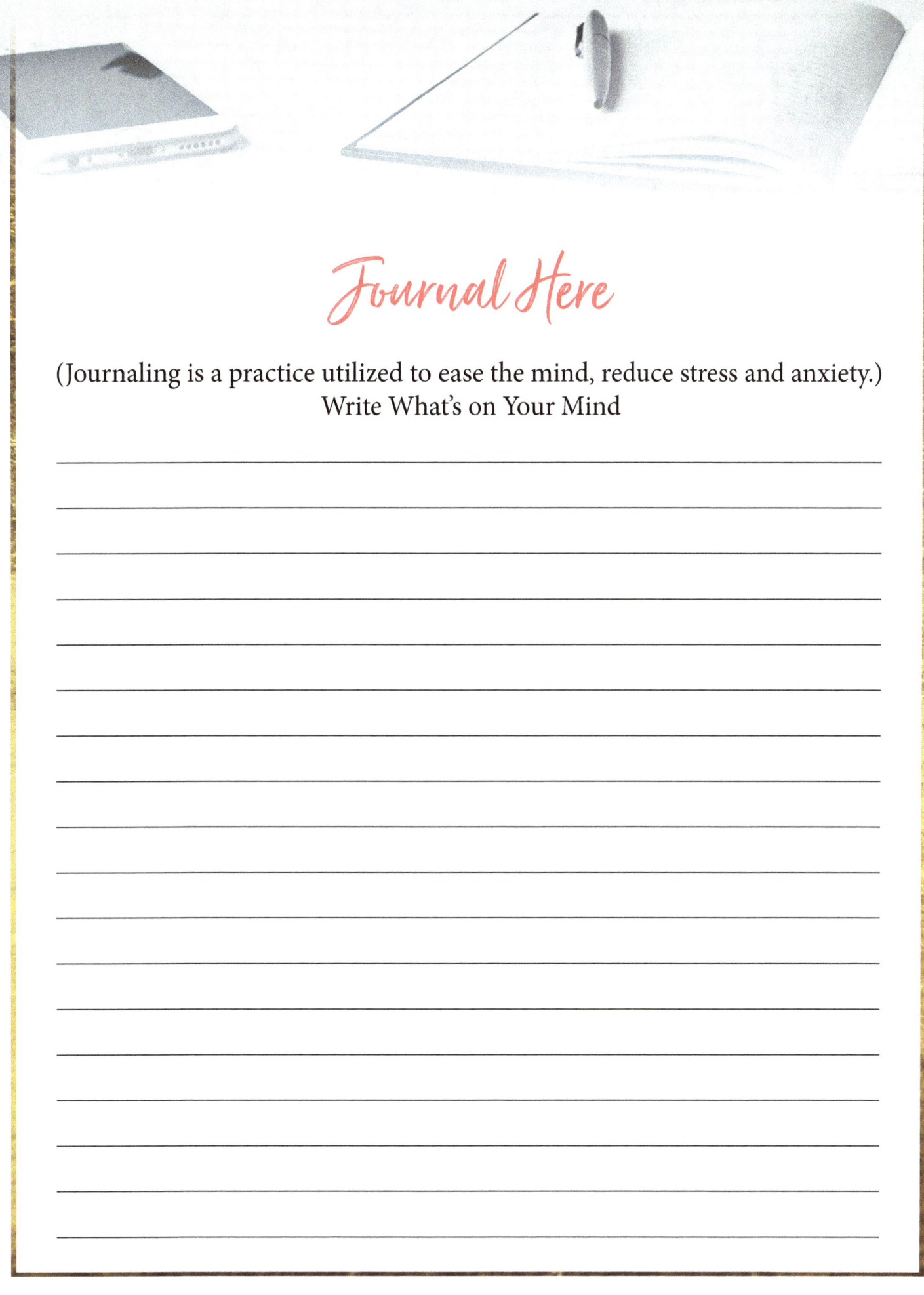

# Journal Here

(Journaling is a practice utilized to ease the mind, reduce stress and anxiety.)
Write What's on Your Mind

_____
_____
_____
_____
_____
_____
_____
_____
_____
_____
_____
_____
_____
_____
_____
_____
_____
_____
_____
_____

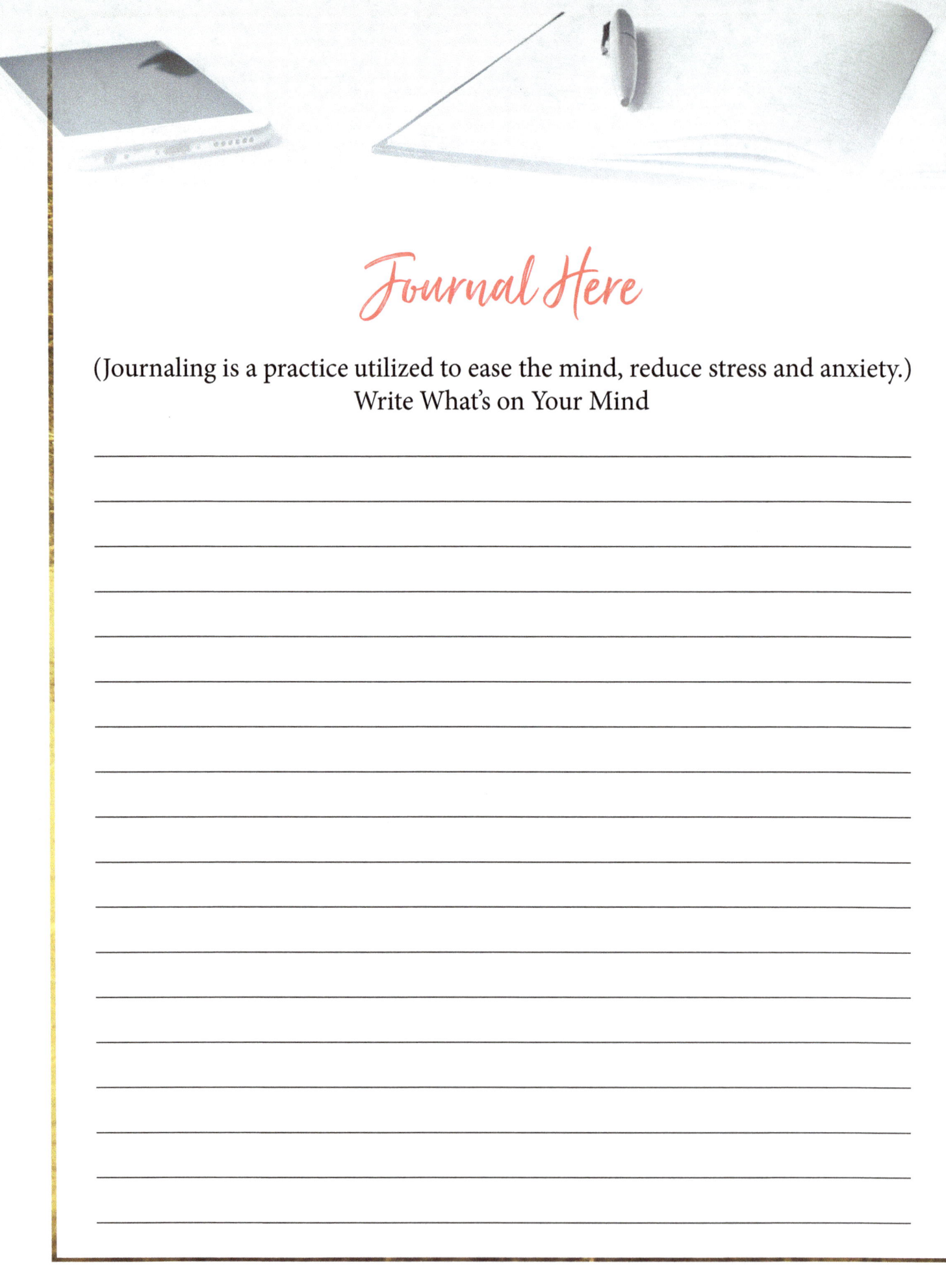

# Journal Here

(Journaling is a practice utilized to ease the mind, reduce stress and anxiety.)
Write What's on Your Mind

_____
_____
_____
_____
_____
_____
_____
_____
_____
_____
_____
_____
_____
_____
_____
_____
_____
_____

# Get My Sh$t Together Vision Board

(Place images or words here that will motivate you to Get your Sh$t together this month)

Month: _____

| SUNDAY | MONDAY | TUESDAY | WEDNESDAY |
|--------|--------|---------|-----------|
|        |        |         |           |
|        |        |         |           |
|        |        |         |           |
|        |        |         |           |
|        |        |         |           |

| THURSDAY | FRIDAY | SATURDAY |

## Notes

# THIS MONTH'S AFFIRMATION

## *I Will Not Allow Anyone or Anything to Get in the Way of Me Living the Life of My Dreams*

### Rewrite & Site

_____

_____

_____

> The will to win, the desire to succeed, the urge to reach your full potential... these are the keys that will unlock the door to personal excellence.
>
> *Confucius*

# Journal Here

(Journaling is a practice utilized to ease the mind, reduce stress and anxiety.)
Write What's on Your Mind

_____
_____
_____
_____
_____
_____
_____
_____
_____
_____
_____
_____
_____
_____
_____
_____

# Journal Here

(Journaling is a practice utilized to ease the mind, reduce stress and anxiety.)
Write What's on Your Mind

_____
_____
_____
_____
_____
_____
_____
_____
_____
_____
_____
_____
_____
_____
_____
_____
_____

# Get My Sh$t Together Vision Board

(Place images or words here that will motivate you to Get your Sh$t together this month)

# Midquarter Get My Sh$T Together Accountability Checklist

Am I on track to Getting My Sh$t together this month?
_____
_____
_____
_____
_____
_____

If yes, what am I doing?
_____
_____
_____
_____
_____
_____

If no what changes do I need to make?
_____
_____
_____
_____
_____
_____
_____

Month: _____

| SUNDAY | MONDAY | TUESDAY | WEDNESDAY |
|---|---|---|---|
| | | | |
| | | | |
| | | | |
| | | | |
| | | | |

| THURSDAY | FRIDAY | SATURDAY |

Notes

# THIS MONTH'S AFFIRMATION

## *I Love who I am and who I am Becoming*

### Rewrite & Site

_____
_____
_____

> *I know where I'm going and I know the truth, and I don't have to be what you want me to be. I'm free to be what I want.*
>
> Muhammad Ali

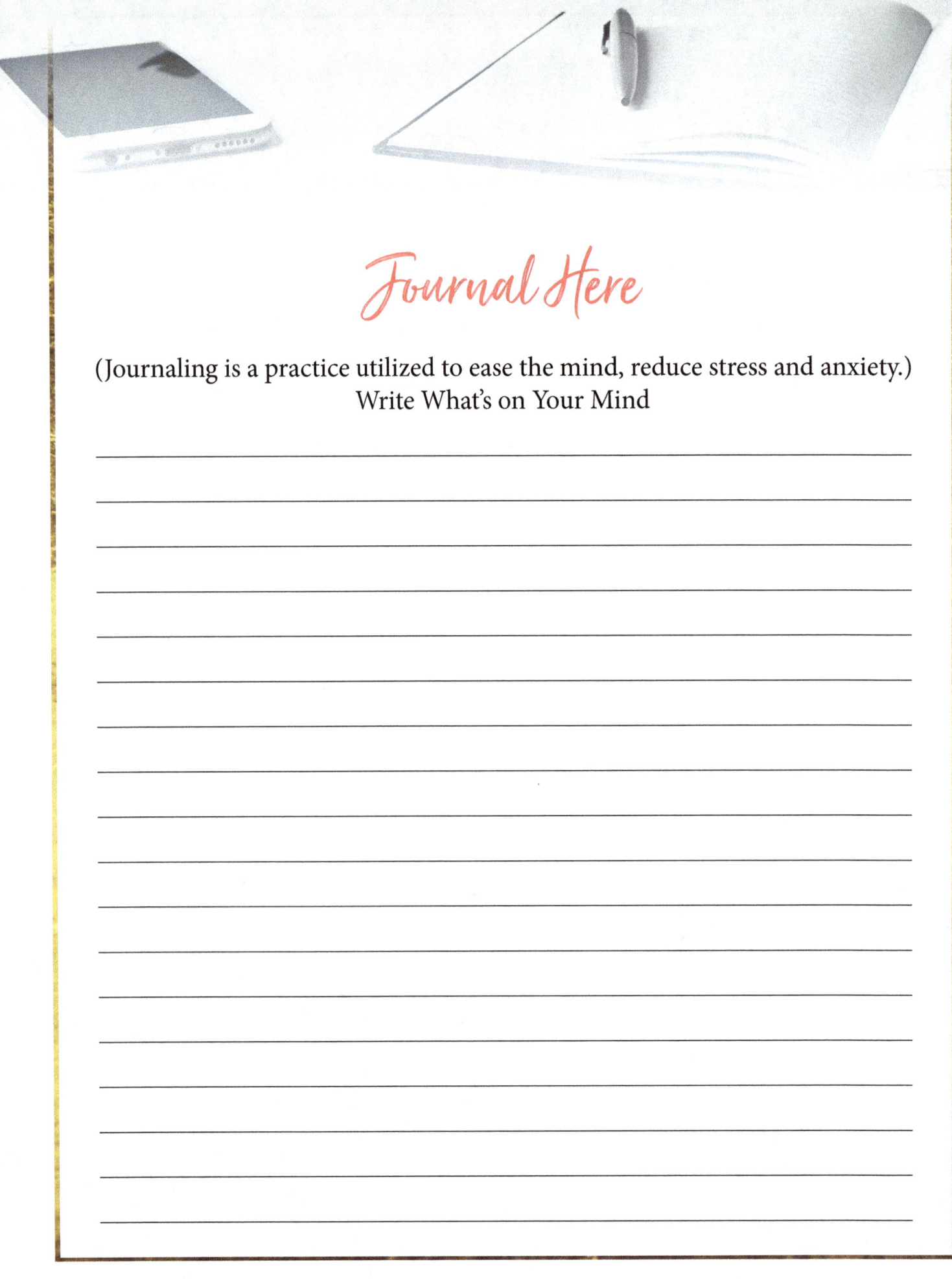

# Journal Here

(Journaling is a practice utilized to ease the mind, reduce stress and anxiety.)
Write What's on Your Mind

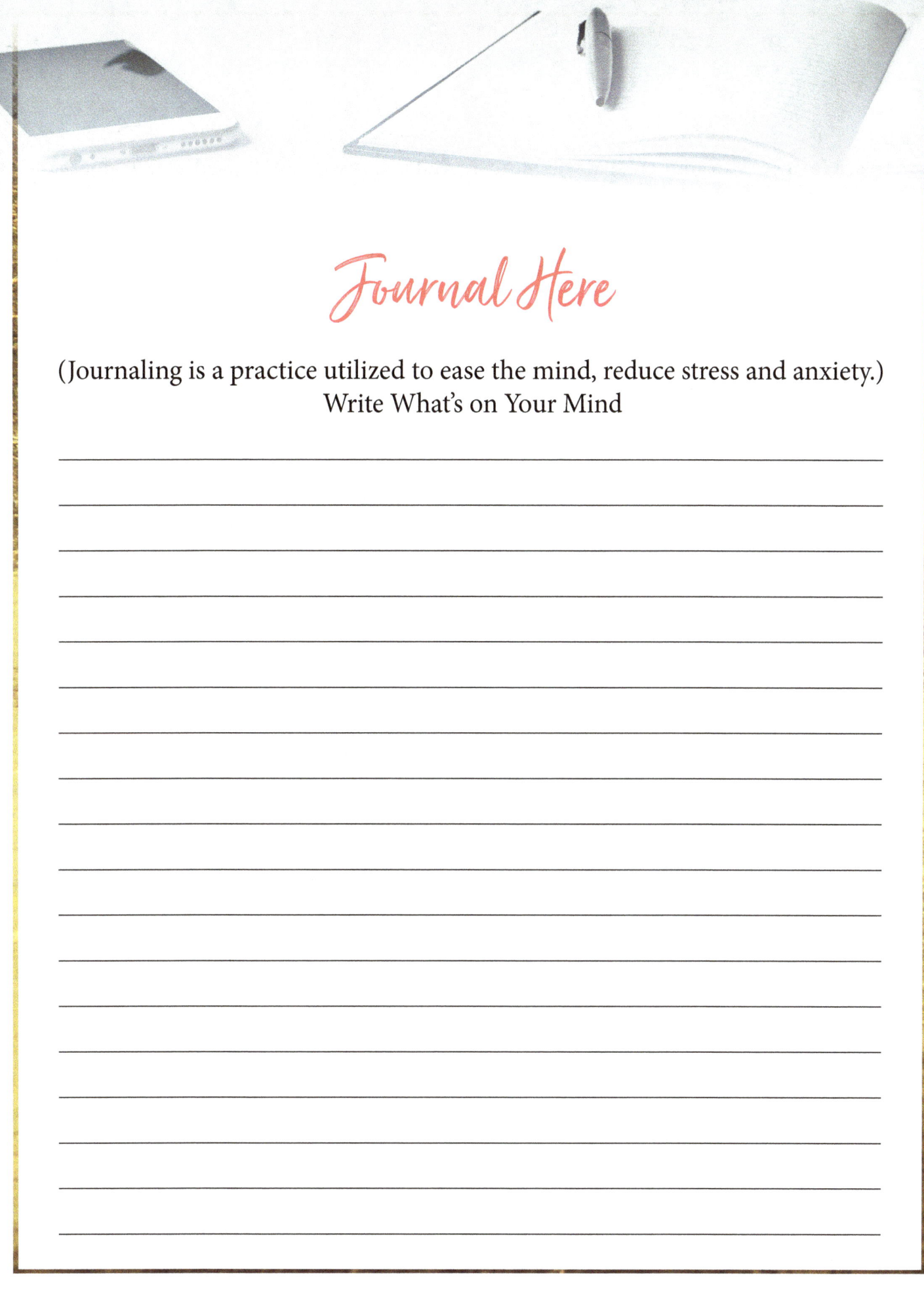

# Journal Here

(Journaling is a practice utilized to ease the mind, reduce stress and anxiety.)
Write What's on Your Mind

# Get My Sh$t Together Vision Board

(Place images or words here that will motivate you to Get your Sh$t together this month)

# 3rd Quarter

# What Sh$T do you need to get together this Quarter?

For example:
- I need to fix my credit.
- I want to get out of depression.
- I want to build a better relationship with my mom.
- I want to lose 20lbs.

_____
_____
_____
_____
_____
_____
_____
_____
_____
_____
_____
_____
_____
_____

# What are the Steps to Getting my Sh$T Together this Quarter?

For example:
- I need to contact that credit company I saw on Instagram.
- I need to go to a physcologist.
- I will call start calling my mom once I week.
- I will stop eating sweets this month.

_____
_____
_____
_____
_____
_____
_____
_____
_____
_____
_____
_____

# What is my Motivation this Quarter to Get My Sh$t Together?

For example:
- I want to buy a house.
- I want to get married.
- I want to start spending Holidays at my parents' house.
- I am going on a girls trip.

# Get My Sh$T Together Word Search

Use this word search puzzle as a way to relax yourself.

## Happiness

```
L J P C Z A M Q G B F H E O H Y R O T C I V M
E I Y L O D N L A E L E V N P Y T R M Q Y P U
R L C U X V O W I D Y N W T P S N E T K P R T
E K N T E A F Y N O I U A R B E E V I G R O T
H A A K M N G N D F N T L A E N M O E P E F R
G R D S A C M O R R G R K E N S N L P R A I I
U R N S F E L I A O C O A A E A I C R W L T U
A I E E L I L T W S O F W S F T A E O A I O M
L V C N K P E A E E L T A Y I I T J G L Z N P
N A S I I X W R R S O I Y S T O T Z R K A K H
Y L A P L N O U S X R H Z T D N A A E O T S X
V W P P L I D T E L S G D R O F Q P S V I T F
V H A A I W T A S T R I K E I R H C S E O F A
A I N H N M A M R W K B B E N Y Y N Y V R N V T
S T S M G V P B M K N O I T I U R F X B S H N
P R O S P E R I T Y E M I N E N C E B O O M D
```

Find the following words in the puzzle.

| | | | |
|---|---|---|---|
| BEATITUDE | DELIRIUM | GLAD | PARADISE |
| BLESSEDNESS | ECSTASY | GLEE | PEACEOFMIND |
| BLISS | ELATION | GOODSPIRITS | PLAY |
| CHEER | ENCHANTMENT | JOY | PLEASURE |
| CHEERFULNESS | ENJOYMENT | JUBILATION | POSITIVE |
| CONTENT | EUPHORIA | LAUGH | PROSPERITY |
| CONTENTMENT | EXHILARATION | LAUGHTER | RAPTURE |
| DELECTATION | FELICITY | MERRY | SMILE |
| DELIGHT | FUN | OPTIMISM | WELLBEING |

Month: _____

| SUNDAY | MONDAY | TUESDAY | WEDNESDAY |
|---|---|---|---|
|  |  |  |  |
|  |  |  |  |
|  |  |  |  |
|  |  |  |  |
|  |  |  |  |

| THURSDAY | FRIDAY | SATURDAY |
|---|---|---|
| | | |
| | | |
| | | |
| | | |
| | | |

## Notes

# THIS MONTH'S AFFIRMATION

## *I Will Keep Going Until I Get that One Yes*

### Rewrite & Site

_____

_____

_____

> *If you can dream it, you can do it.*

*Walt Disney*

# Journal Here

(Journaling is a practice utilized to ease the mind, reduce stress and anxiety.)
Write What's on Your Mind

# Journal Here

(Journaling is a practice utilized to ease the mind, reduce stress and anxiety.)
Write What's on Your Mind

_____
_____
_____
_____
_____
_____
_____
_____
_____
_____
_____
_____
_____
_____
_____
_____
_____
_____

# Get My Sh$t Together Vision Board

(Place images or words here that will motivate you to Get your Sh$t together this month)

Month: _____

| SUNDAY | MONDAY | TUESDAY | WEDNESDAY |
|--------|--------|---------|-----------|
|        |        |         |           |
|        |        |         |           |
|        |        |         |           |
|        |        |         |           |
|        |        |         |           |

| THURSDAY | FRIDAY | SATURDAY |
|---|---|---|
| | | |
| | | |
| | | |
| | | |
| | | |

## Notes

THIS MONTH'S AFFIRMATION

## I am a Gift to the World and Everyone I Encounter

### Rewrite & Site

_____

_____

_____

> *Do the one thing you think you cannot do. Fail at it. Try again. Do better the second time. The only people who never tumble are those who never mount the high wire. This is your moment. Own it.*
>
> Oprah Winfrey

# Journal Here

(Journaling is a practice utilized to ease the mind, reduce stress and anxiety.)
Write What's on Your Mind

_____
_____
_____
_____
_____
_____
_____
_____
_____
_____
_____
_____
_____
_____
_____
_____
_____
_____

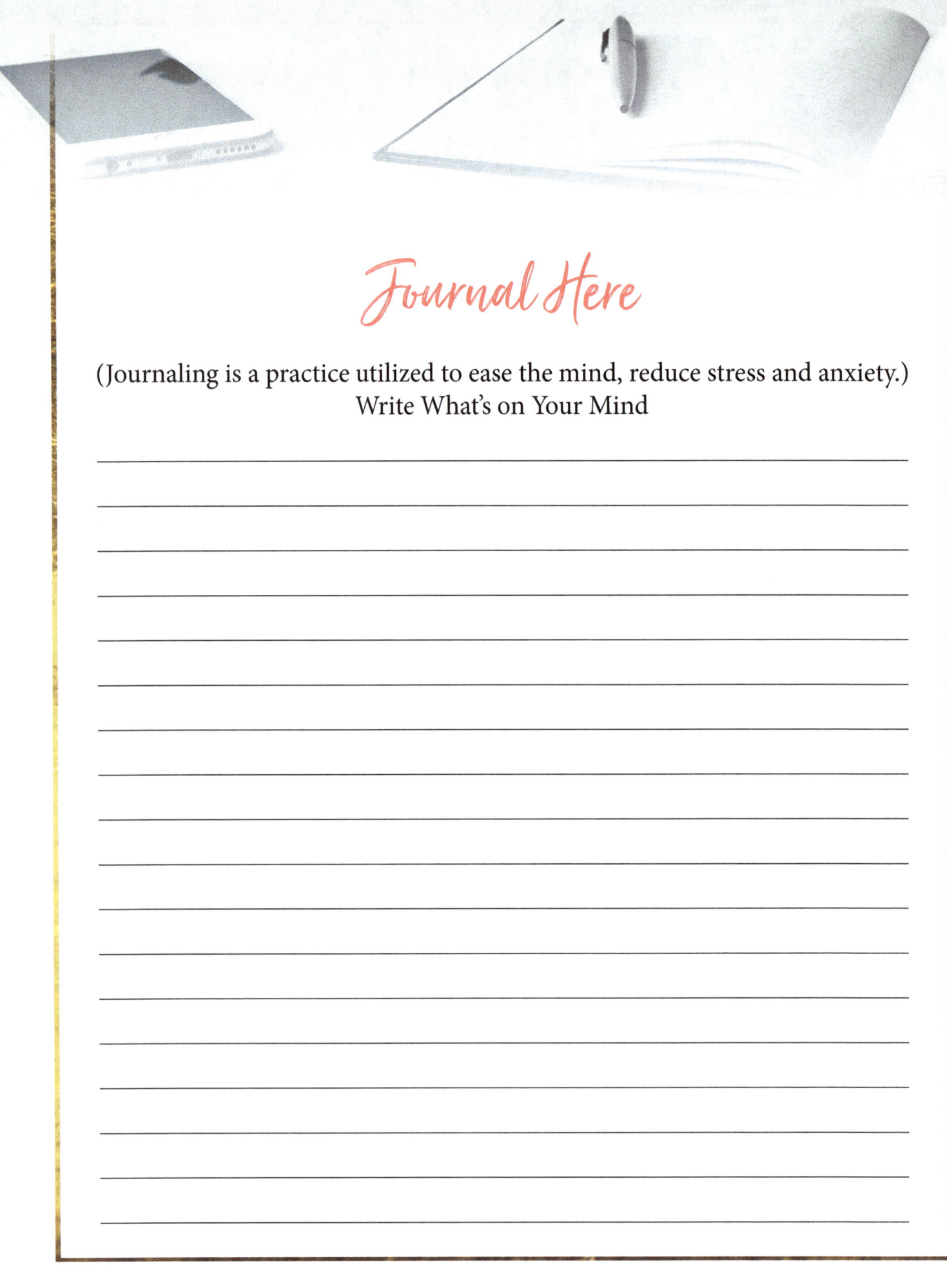

# Journal Here

(Journaling is a practice utilized to ease the mind, reduce stress and anxiety.)
Write What's on Your Mind

# Get My Sh$t Together Vision Board

(Place images or words here that will motivate you to Get your Sh$t together this month)

# Midquarter Get My Sh$T Together Accountability Checklist

Am I on track to Getting My Sh$t together this month?
_____
_____
_____
_____
_____
_____

If yes, what am I doing?
_____
_____
_____
_____
_____
_____

If no what changes do I need to make?
_____
_____
_____
_____
_____
_____
_____
_____

Month: _____

| SUNDAY | MONDAY | TUESDAY | WEDNESDAY |
|--------|--------|---------|-----------|
|        |        |         |           |
|        |        |         |           |
|        |        |         |           |
|        |        |         |           |
|        |        |         |           |

| THURSDAY | FRIDAY | SATURDAY |
|----------|--------|----------|
|          |        |          |
|          |        |          |
|          |        |          |
|          |        |          |
|          |        |          |

## Notes

THIS MONTH'S AFFIRMATION

# I Create My Own Happiness

## Rewrite & Site

_____

_____

_____

> **We may encounter many defeats but we must not be defeated.**
>
> *Maya Angelou*

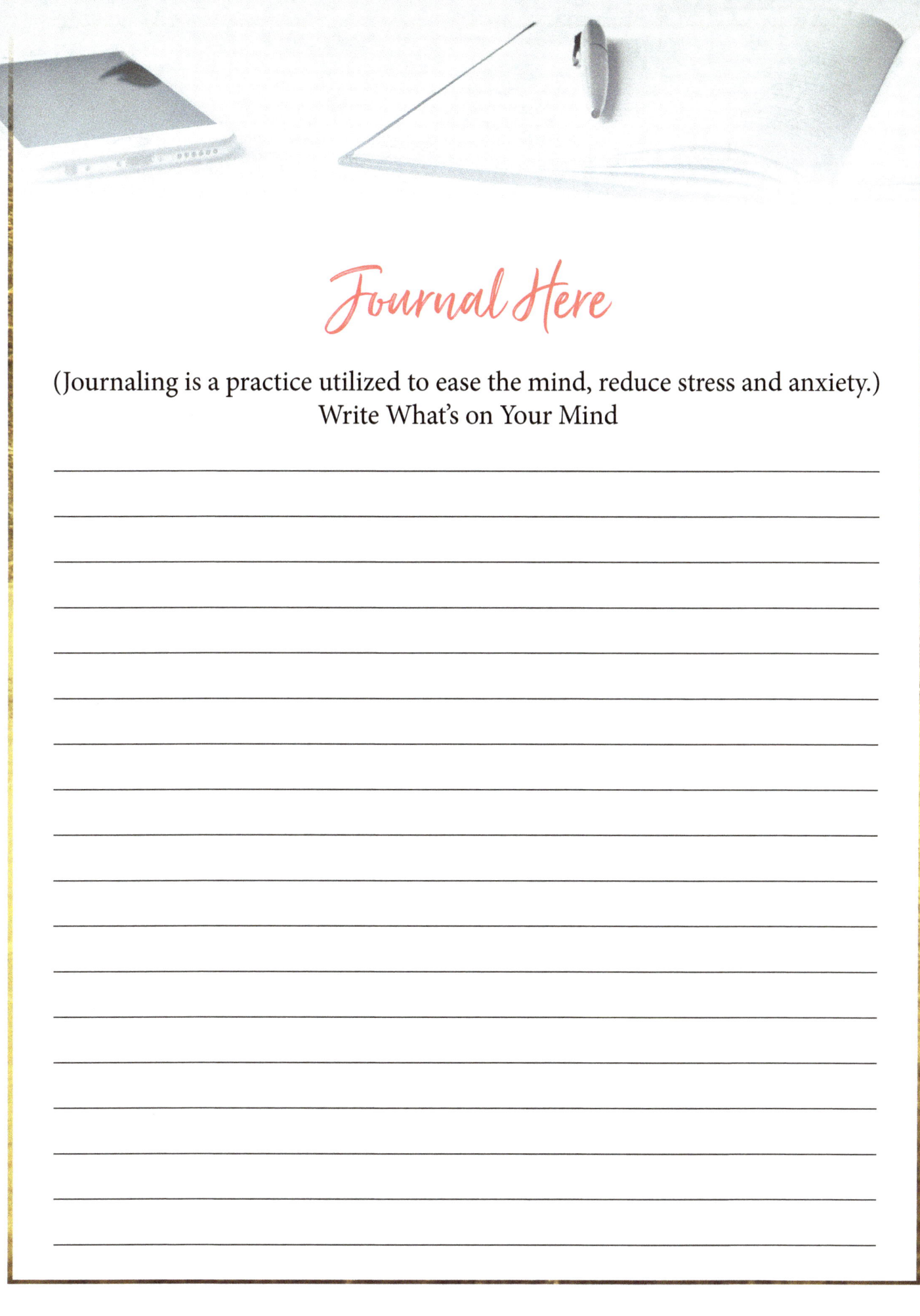

# Journal Here

(Journaling is a practice utilized to ease the mind, reduce stress and anxiety.)
Write What's on Your Mind

_____
_____
_____
_____
_____
_____
_____
_____
_____
_____
_____
_____
_____
_____
_____
_____
_____

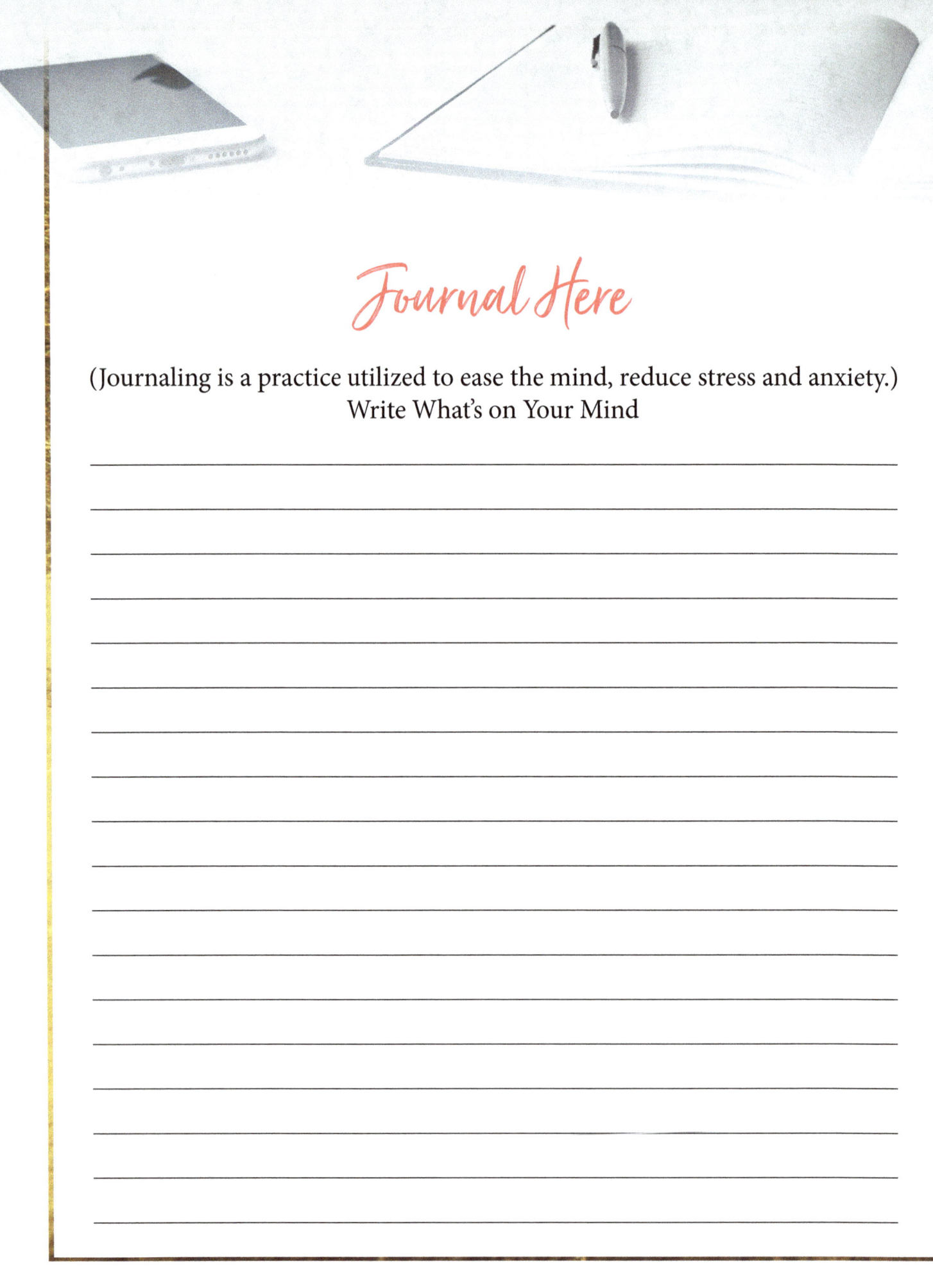

# Journal Here

(Journaling is a practice utilized to ease the mind, reduce stress and anxiety.)
Write What's on Your Mind

# Get My Sh$t Together Vision Board

(Place images or words here that will motivate you to Get your Sh$t together this month)

# 4th Quarter

# What Sh$T do you need to get together this Quarter?

For example:
- I need to fix my credit.
- I want to get out of depression.
- I want to build a better relationship with my mom.
- I want to lose 20lbs.

_____
_____
_____
_____
_____
_____
_____
_____
_____
_____
_____
_____
_____
_____
_____
_____

# What are the Steps to Getting my Sh$T Together this Quarter?

For example:
- I need to contact that credit company I saw on Instagram.
- I need to go to a physcologist.
- I will call start calling my mom once I week.
- I will stop eating sweets this month.

_____
_____
_____
_____
_____
_____
_____
_____
_____
_____
_____
_____

# What is my Motivation this Quarter to Get My Sh$t Together?

For example:
- I want to buy a house.
- I want to get married.
- I want to start spending Holidays at my parents' house.
- I am going on a girls trip.

# Get My Sh$T Together Word Search

Use this word search puzzle as a way to relax yourself.

## Peace

```
L J P C Z A M Q G B F H E O H Y R O T C I V M
E I Y L O D N L A E L E V N P Y T R M Q Y P U
R L C U X V O W I D Y N W T P S N E T K P R T
E K N T E A F Y N O I U A R B E E V I G R O T
H A A K M N G N D F N T L A E N M O E P E F R
G R D S A C M O R R G R K E N S N L P R A I I
U R N S F E L I A O C O A A E A I C R W L T U
A I E E L I L T W S O F W S F T A E O A I O M
L V C N K P E A E E L T A Y I I T J G L Z N O
N A S I I X W R R S O I Y S T O T Z R K A K H
Y L A P L N O U S X R H Z T D N A A E O T S X
V W P P L I D T E L S G D R O F Q P S V I T F
V H A A I W T A S T R I K E I R H C S E O F A
A I N H N M A M R W K B B E N Y Y N V R N V T
S T S M G V P B M K N O I T I U R F X B S H N
P R O S P E R I T Y E M I N E N C E B O O M D
```

Find the following words in the puzzle.

| | | |
|---|---|---|
| RECONCILIATION | PACIFISM | AMITY |
| CONCILIATION | CALMNESS | QUIET |
| PACIFICATION | SERENITY | ORDER |
| TRANQUILITY | PRIVACY | STILL |
| FRIENDSHIP | SILENCE | PEACE |
| CESSATION | TREATY | CALM |
| STABILITY | ACCORD | HUSH |
| PATIENCE | UNITY | |

Month: _____

| SUNDAY | MONDAY | TUESDAY | WEDNESDAY |
|--------|--------|---------|-----------|
|        |        |         |           |
|        |        |         |           |
|        |        |         |           |
|        |        |         |           |
|        |        |         |           |

| THURSDAY | FRIDAY | SATURDAY |
|----------|--------|----------|
|  |  |  |
|  |  |  |
|  |  |  |
|  |  |  |
|  |  |  |

## Notes

# THIS MONTH'S AFFIRMATION

## I Am Happy & Successful

### Rewrite & Site

_____

_____

_____

> *Life is 10% what happens to you and 90% how you react to it. If you don't like how things are, change it! You're not a tree.*
>
> Jim Rohn

# Journal Here

(Journaling is a practice utilized to ease the mind, reduce stress and anxiety.)
Write What's on Your Mind

_____
_____
_____
_____
_____
_____
_____
_____
_____
_____
_____
_____
_____
_____
_____
_____
_____

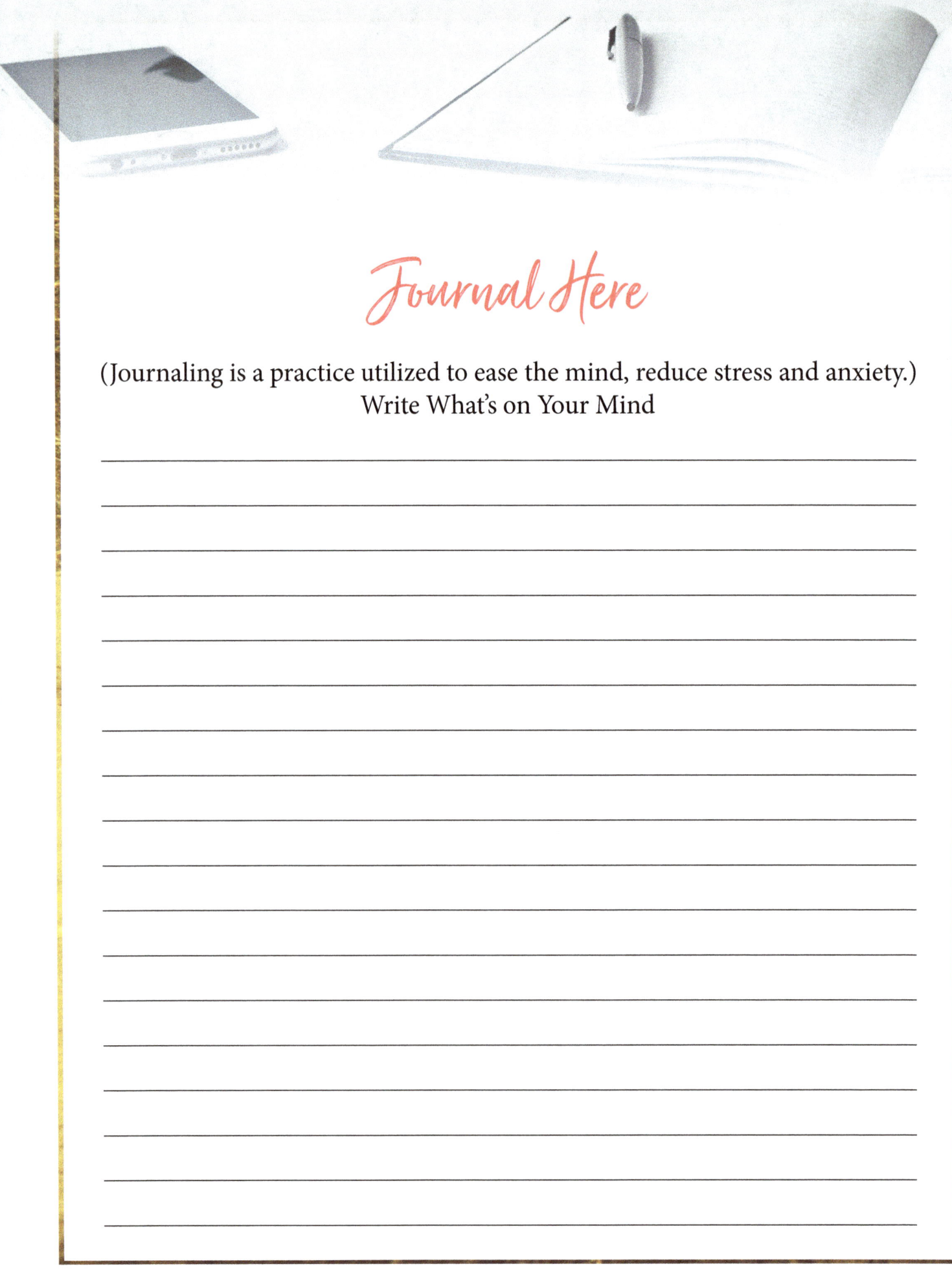

# Journal Here

(Journaling is a practice utilized to ease the mind, reduce stress and anxiety.)
Write What's on Your Mind

_____
_____
_____
_____
_____
_____
_____
_____
_____
_____
_____
_____
_____
_____
_____

# Get My Sh$t Together Vision Board

(Place images or words here that will motivate you to Get your Sh$t together this month)

Month: _____

| SUNDAY | MONDAY | TUESDAY | WEDNESDAY |
|--------|--------|---------|-----------|
|        |        |         |           |
|        |        |         |           |
|        |        |         |           |
|        |        |         |           |
|        |        |         |           |

| THURSDAY | FRIDAY | SATURDAY |
|---|---|---|
| | | |
| | | |
| | | |
| | | |
| | | |

## Notes

# THIS MONTH'S AFFIRMATION

## I am Healthy & Wealthy

## Rewrite & Site

_____

_____

_____

> *There is no passion to be found playing small - in settling for a life that is less than the one you are capable of living.*
>
> Nelson Mandela

# Journal Here

(Journaling is a practice utilized to ease the mind, reduce stress and anxiety.)
Write What's on Your Mind

_____
_____
_____
_____
_____
_____
_____
_____
_____
_____
_____
_____
_____
_____
_____
_____

# Journal Here

(Journaling is a practice utilized to ease the mind, reduce stress and anxiety.)
Write What's on Your Mind

_____
_____
_____
_____
_____
_____
_____
_____
_____
_____
_____
_____
_____
_____
_____
_____
_____
_____
_____
_____

# Get My Sh$t Together Vision Board

(Place images or words here that will motivate you to Get your Sh$t together this month)

# Midquarter Get My Sh$T Together Accountability Checklist

Am I on track to Getting My Sh$t together this month?
_____
_____
_____
_____
_____
_____
_____

If yes, what am I doing?
_____
_____
_____
_____
_____
_____
_____

If no what changes do I need to make?
_____
_____
_____
_____
_____
_____
_____
_____

Month: _____

| SUNDAY | MONDAY | TUESDAY | WEDNESDAY |
|--------|--------|---------|-----------|
|        |        |         |           |
|        |        |         |           |
|        |        |         |           |
|        |        |         |           |
|        |        |         |           |

| THURSDAY | FRIDAY | SATURDAY |

# Notes

# THIS MONTH'S AFFIRMATION

## *I am Strong & Determined*

### Rewrite & Site

_____

_____

_____

# Journal Here

(Journaling is a practice utilized to ease the mind, reduce stress and anxiety.)
Write What's on Your Mind

_____
_____
_____
_____
_____
_____
_____
_____
_____
_____
_____
_____
_____
_____
_____
_____
_____
_____
_____

# Journal Here

(Journaling is a practice utilized to ease the mind, reduce stress and anxiety.)
Write What's on Your Mind

_____
_____
_____
_____
_____
_____
_____
_____
_____
_____
_____
_____
_____
_____
_____
_____
_____

# Get My Sh$t Together Vision Board

(Place images or words here that will motivate you to Get your Sh$t together this month)

Interested in Writing and/or Publishing a Book/Journal?
Visit www.A2ZBookspublishing.net

www.ingramcontent.com/pod-product-compliance
Lightning Source LLC
Chambersburg PA
CBHW081752100526
44592CB00015B/2403